Around Shetland ...

FAIR ISLE
1. North Haven and Sheep Rock, Fair Isle.
2. A quiet moment, Fair Isle.
3. Dronger and the North Light, Fair Isle.
4. Sheep-shearing, Fair Isle.

SOUTH MAINLAND
5. Sumburgh.
6. Sumburgh Lighthouse.
7. Jarlshof.
8. St Ninian's Isle chapel and beach.
9. St Ninian's Isle.
10. Spiggie Bay.
11. Crofthouse Museum, Dunrossness.
12. Hoswick, Sandwick.
13. Leebitton, Sandwick.
14. Mousa Broch.
15. Aith Voe, Cunningsburgh.
16. Corn work, Cunningsburgh.
17. Easter Quarff.
18. Gulberwick.
19. Hamnavoe, Burra Isle.
20. Meal Beach, Burra Isle.
21. Bridge End, Burra Isle.
22. South Havra.

LERWICK
23. Aerial view of Lerwick.
24. Lerwick from the Knab.
25. Skipidock.
26. King George V Park.
27. Market Cross.
28. South End.
29. Lerwick Harbour.

CENTRAL MAINLAND
30. Scalloway.
31. Blacksness, Scalloway.
32. Muckle Haa garden, Scalloway.
33. Tingwall Manse.
34. Gletness.
35. Wormadale.
36. Weisdale Voe.
37. Vidlin.

WEST MAINLAND
38. Tresta.
39. Twatt, Bixter.
40. Aith.
41. Lunklet Burn.
42. Skeld Voe.
43. Croft house, Bridge of Walls.
44. Walls.
45. Greenton, Walls.
46. Burrastow House.
47. Bousta, Sandness.
48. Sandness Mills.

NOR
49. Muckle Roe.
50. Land Ayre, Northmavine.
51. Hillswick.
52. The Drongs.
53. Eshaness.
54. Heylor, Ronas Voe.
55. North Roe.
56. Point of Fethaland.

THE ISLES
57. Gaada Stack, Foula.
58. Shetland ponies, Foula.
59. North House, Papa Stour.
60. Papa Stour.
61. Maiden Stacks, Papa Stour.
62. Out Skerries.
63. Drying fish, Skerries.
64. Out Skerries.
65. Symbister, Whalsay.
66. Bressay.
67. Fetlar.
68. Old Haa, Burravoe, Yell.
69. Breckon, Yell.
70. St Olaf's Church, Unst.
71. Shetland ponies at Uyeasound, Unst.
72. Hermaness, Unst.
73. Muckle Flugga.

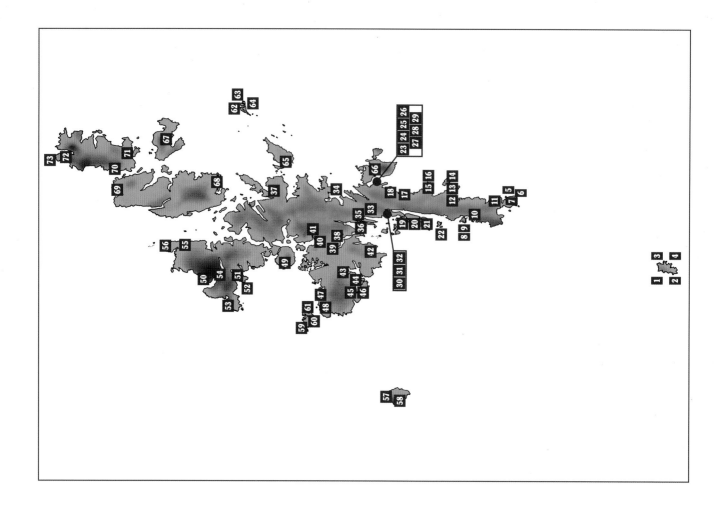

1. North Haven and Sheep Rock, Fair Isle, with the ferry *Good Shepherd IV*.

© *Hugh Harrop*

2. A quiet moment, Fair Isle.

3. Dronger and the North Light, Fair Isle. The North Light was commissioned in 1892 and had a sundial to check lighting times.

© *Paul Turner*

4. Sheep-shearing at Fair Isle.

© Colin Wilson

5. Sumburgh looking towards Foula.

6. Sumburgh Lighthouse, built in 1821 by Thomas Stevenson, father of Robert Louis Stevenson.

© *Colin Ganson*

7. Jarlshof. The site dates back 3000 years and is many layered, with settlements from Neolithic dwellings to a 16th century laird's house.

© Paul Turner

8. The ruins of the 12th century chapel at St Ninian's Isle, and the best example of a tombolo of shell sand in Europe. © *Paul Turner*

9. St Ninian's Isle was once tidal, and populated until 1700 when the peat supply ran out.

10. Spiggie Bay.

© Colin Wilson

11. Crofthouse Museum, Voe, Dunrossness, was built in 1870. Today it offers a glimpse of a crofting life in former times. © *Hansen Black*

12. Hoswick, Sandwick.

13. Leebitton, Sandwick, and the 17th century mansion of Sand Lodge, home of the Bruce family.

© *Colin Ganson*

14. Mousa Broch, built in the Iron Age. The best preserved broch in Britain, standing over 42 feet high.

15. M.V. *St Sunniva* passes Aith Voe, Cunningsburgh.

16. Corn work, Cunningsburgh.

© *Jim Nicolson*

17. Easter Quarff.

18. Gulberwick.

19. Hamnavoe, Burra Isle.

20. Meal Beach, Burra.

© Kieran Murray

21. Bridge End, Burra Isle.

22. South Havra lies south of Burra. Once home to eight families, the island was abandoned in 1923.

© *Colin Ganson*

23. Aerial view of Lerwick. Sound in the foreground.

24. Lerwick from the Knab.

27. Market Cross, Lerwick.

28. South End, Lerwick. The Knowe with a boat as its garage roof, and the Widows Homes, originally built by Arthur Anderson in 1865.

© *Colin Ganson*

29. Lerwick Harbour during the Cutty Sark Tall Ships' Races visit in 1999.

© *Kieran Murray*

30. Shetland's ancient capital, Scalloway.

31. Blacksness, Scalloway, and the ruins of Scalloway Castle (built in 1600).

© Colin Ganson

32. Muckle Haa garden, Scalloway, in full bloom.

© Helen Harrison

33. Tingwall Manse in the fertile Tingwall valley and the loch with nesting swans.

© *Colin Wilson*

34. Gletness.

35. Wormadale.

36. Weisdale Voe with Kalliness, Sound, and an old planticrub in the foreground.

© *Andy Gear*

37. Vidlin.

38. Tresta.

39. Twatt, Bixter.

40. Aith.

41. Lunklet Burn.

© Colin Ganson

42. Skeld Voe.

43. Croft house, Bridge of Walls.

44. Walls.

45. Greenton, Walls.

46. Burrastow House, Walls.

© Colin Ganson

47. Bousta, Sandness.

© Colin Wilson

48. Sandness Mills.

49. Muckle Roe – 'The Big Red Isle' consists of red granite some 350 million years old.

© *Colin Wilson*

50. Lang Ayre, Northmavine.

51. Hillswick, dominated by St Magnus Hotel.

© *Colin Ganson*

52. Sunset over the Drongs, Eshaness.

© *Paul Turner*

53. Winter gale, Eshaness.

© Alan Gair

54. Heylor, Ronas Voe.

55. North Roe.

56. The point of Fethaland, once the busiest haaf station in Shetland with sixty sixareens and twenty lodges for shore accommodation.

57. Gaada Stack and North Coast, Foula.

58. Shetland ponies on the Noup, Foula.

59. North House and Housa Voe, Papa Stour.

© Paul Turner

60. Papa Stour.

61. Maiden Stacks, Papa Stour.

© *Paul Turner*

62. Out Skerries.

63. Drying salted fish, Skerries.

64. The three main islands of Out Skerries. In the foreground is Housay, joined to Bruray by a bridge, and Grunay. © *Kieran Murray*

65. Symbister, Whalsay. Pier House, a Hanseatic Böd used by German merchants, stands in the foreground.　　　　© Colin Ganson

66. Maryfield, Bressay.

67. Fetlar and the SOLI (Society of Our Lady of the Isles), or more commonly "The Nuns", complex. The headland of lambhoga juts out from the right.

© *John Coutts*

68. Old Haa, Burravoe, Yell. One of Yell's oldest buildings (1672), now a visitor centre with displays of local interest.   © Andy Gear

69. Breckon, Yell.

© Colin Wilson

70. St Olaf's Church, Lundawick, Unst.

71. Shetland ponies at Uyeasound, Unst.

72. Hermaness, Unst. Nature reserve for 100,000 breeding birds.

73. Muckle Flugga, the most northerly point in Britain, from Hermaness, Unst. The lighthouse was built by David Stevenson in 1858.

© *Michael Steciuk*